The

FIRST **100**STRUMMING
PATTERNS**FOR**GUITAR

The Beginner's Guide to Strumming on Guitar and Playing in Time

JOSEPH**ALEXANDER**

FUNDAMENTAL**CHANGES**

The First 100 Strumming Patterns for Guitar

The Beginner's Guide to Strumming on Guitar and Playing in Time

Published by **www.fundamental-changes.com**

ISBN: 978-1-78933-395-4

Copyright © 2022 Joseph Alexander

Edited by Tim Pettingale

www.fundamental-changes.com

Join our free Facebook Community of Cool Musicians

www.facebook.com/groups/fundamentalguitar

Instagram: **FundamentalChanges**

For over 350 Free Guitar Lessons with Videos Check Out

www.fundamental-changes.com

Cover Image Copyright: Shutterstock

Contents

About the Author

Joseph Alexander is one of the most prolific writers of modern guitar tuition methods.

He has sold over 1,000,000 books that have educated and inspired a generation of upcoming musicians. His uncomplicated tuition style is based around breaking down the barriers between theory and performance, and making music accessible to all.

Educated at London's Guitar Institute and Leeds College of Music, where he earned a degree in Jazz Studies, Joseph has taught thousands of students and written over 40 books on playing the guitar.

He is the managing director of *Fundamental Changes Ltd.*, a publishing company whose sole purpose is to create the highest quality music tuition books and pay excellent royalties to writers and musicians.

Fundamental Changes has published over 170 music tuition books and is currently accepting submissions from prospective authors and teachers of all instruments. Get in touch via **webcontact@fundamental-changes.com** if you'd like to work with us on a project.

Introduction

Confident rhythm and strumming are at the core of everything you'll ever do on the guitar, and in fact it's probably what you'll spend 90% of your time playing as a guitarist.

We might spend hours in the practice room working on our technique, scales and soloing but ask yourself when you last heard anything other than a short guitar solo on mainstream radio.

I grew up listening to musicians like Van Halen, Steve Vai, Joe Satriani, Guns N' Roses and Metallica, so rock solos are a part of my identity as a guitarist, but even so, take a moment to listen to any great instrumental rock band and you'll hear that almost every solo, and every song is built on a foundation of great rhythm guitar performed with accurate strumming and creative arrangements.

Whether you want to play pop, rock, jazz, blues or country you need to master accurate strumming, lock into the groove and build a solid platform that allows the other instruments to shine.

Guitarists are notorious for wanting to take the big solo and grab the spotlight, but for most players that'll only ever be 1% of the gig. The other 99% is all about playing the rhythm part perfectly and being part of the band.

Every baseball player wants to knock it out of the park, but they'll actually spend the vast majority of their time out in the field. As an Englishman who grew up playing cricket – a game that can last five days and end in a draw – I can totally empathise with this!

When you can play rhythm guitar properly, you'll be a huge asset to any band, and are much more likely to get hired than the guy that can only solo. When your strumming is solid, the drums and bass can stop worrying about keeping time and play more creatively as musicians. This vastly improves the music you make and adds a whole new dimension to your band. Always remember that it's not the drummer's job to keep time – it's *everyone's* job! If you can master great strumming and tight rhythm, you'll always be in demand as a musician.

If you're more interested in playing guitar to accompany yourself in a "singer-songwriter" style of music, then playing great rhythm with confidence and nuance is even more important. In this setup, there's nowhere to hide so you're going to want to master your strumming skills early. Good strumming = good rhythm, and there's nothing worse than a player whose music speeds up or slows down uncontrollably.

Whether you're just starting out or have been playing a while, time spent developing an accurate, confident strumming technique will set you apart as a musician and dramatically improve your playing.

This book starts from first principles but even if you've been playing a while, please don't skip forward because everything that comes later is built on these rock-solid foundations.

When you've worked through this book, you'll have a newfound confidence and understanding of rhythm guitar, and plenty of insight into how to play folk, rock, pop, jazz, funk and blues.

We'll begin with four golden rules that apply in every style of music, learn how to hold the pick, then discover the secrets of how to strum *any* rhythm.

Once we've built that foundation together, we'll move on to applying these essential skills to the most important types of music to help you build a repertoire of rhythms that work every time. These will be the perfect springboard for you to get creative and write your own songs.

Ready? Grab your guitar and let's dive in.

Have fun!

Joseph

Get the Audio

The audio files for this book are available to download for free from **www.fundamental-changes.com.** The link is in the top right-hand corner. Click on the "Guitar" link then simply select this book title from the drop-down menu and follow the instructions to get the audio.

We recommend that you download the files directly to your computer, not to your tablet, and extract them there before adding them to your media library. You can then put them onto your tablet, iPod or burn them to CD. On the download page there are instructions and we also provide technical support via the contact form.

For over 350 free guitar lessons with videos check out:

www.fundamental-changes.com

Join our free Facebook Community of Cool Musicians

www.facebook.com/groups/fundamentalguitar

Tag us for a share on Instagram: **FundamentalChanges**

Chapter One: Fundamental Strumming Patterns

If you want to get better at strumming very quickly there are four golden rules you should always follow. They are:

- Tap your foot on the beat

- When your foot goes down, your strumming hand goes down

- When your foot comes up, your strumming hand comes up

- Use a metronome and record yourself regularly

You might be wondering how and why you should do all these things. Let's start with tapping your foot.

The thing is, sound is just a load of wobbly air waves that hit your ear drums. Your brain then processes those waves into music, speech or traffic noise – whatever the sound may be. While for most people it's easy to *hear* music, there's actually very little *physical* connection with it.

All music has a *pulse* or *beat*, and making great music is all about connecting physically to this beat. The best way to move music from vibrations in the air to being a physical part of you is to move your body to it, and what better way to do this than to tap your foot on the beat.

We will discuss this idea in more detail soon, but *most* music has four beats in each *measure* or *bar*. That's why drummers often count in "one two three four" before the start of a song – to help everyone in the band feel the pulse before they've even played a note. It's a way to connect the band and make sure everyone begins the song perfectly in time.

I could pick about 90% of rock songs to demonstrate this point, but go on YouTube and check out the video to *Smells Like Teen Spirit* by Nirvana here:

https://youtu.be/hTWKbfoikeg

The video conveniently begins with a close up of someone tapping their foot in time with the song. Copy that movement and see if you can keep your foot tapping in time throughout the whole song. When you're done, check out your other favourite tracks and see if you can tap your foot to the beat all the way through.

This might seem like a strange instruction to get at the beginning of a book on strumming, but the truth is that you need to learn to feel the rhythm of any song before you can play it in time. You need to turn the pulse of the song into a physical movement because playing guitar is a *physical* act, and the strums you make will *lock into* the physical movement of your foot.

So, now we know that tapping your foot in time to the music connects you physically to the beat, but let's learn how that movement helps you become a better rhythm guitarist. It's really quite simple! Don't worry, I promise you'll be making music soon!

You may have heard the phrases *down beat* and *up beat* before, but you may not know that they relate directly to music. The rhythmic pulse we described above is the down beat. Your foot taps *down* and hits the floor on the *down beat* of the music.

The great thing is that the down-up movement of your hand when you're strumming will normally mirror the down-up movement of your foot. If your foot's moving in time, your strums will always be in time. In fact, your whole body will be synchronised in time with the music and you'll never have to *think* about the rhythm of the song, you will genuinely feel it in your body and everything you play will be in time.

The fourth golden rule is to always use a metronome when you play and record yourself regularly. Here's why!

When we first start playing the guitar, our most immediate concerns are to develop the basic physical movements that allow us to play clean-sounding notes and chords. Often, there's not much awareness of the concept of playing "in time". However, if you have a metronome clicking while you practice, you'll naturally start to develop an awareness of playing in time. In this book, we're going to look at a lot of exercises you can do with a metronome to develop great strumming and timekeeping, but for now, download a metronome app on your phone and have a play around so you understand its main features.

How to Hold the Pick

Next, let's take a quick look at the best way to hold the pick for control and accuracy. As a teacher, one of the most common mistakes I see in beginner students is holding the pick incorrectly. When the pick isn't held properly it's like trying to write by holding a pen right at the top. You have no control and your handwriting ends up being pretty terrible.

The secret is to hold the pick with the pad of the thumb and the *side* of the index finger (not the pad). You should only have about 1/8th of an inch (a couple of millimetres) of the pick sticking out below the thumb. Copy the position in the diagram below. It might feel a little strange at first, if you're used to holding the pick another way, but stick with it.

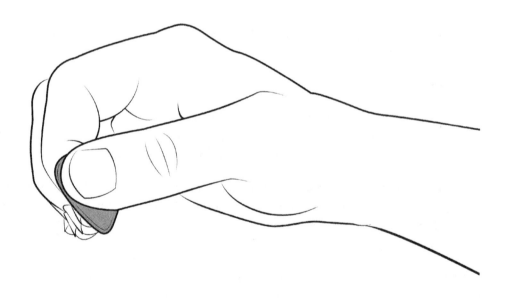

Where to Strum

Where you physically strum the guitar is a matter of personal taste and depends on the kind of sound you want to create.

If you strum near the bridge of the guitar the sound will be quite thin and trebly. If you strum near the neck your sound will be much warmer. Both sounds are useful for different things, but I suggest you start by placing your strumming hand either directly over the sound hole on an acoustic guitar, or between the middle and neck pickups on a Strat-style guitar (as below).

Keep your wrist soft and loose and keep your arm parallel to the guitar body. It's a common habit to raise your elbow away from the guitar body which is bad because it creates an uncomfortable angle and tension in your wrist.

Also, the strumming movement comes from the *wrist*, not the arm. Think about turning your wrist to brush the strings with the pick, rather than moving your arm up and down. Your elbow should stay more or less in the same place.

The images below show the natural resting position of the strumming arm on an electric guitar.

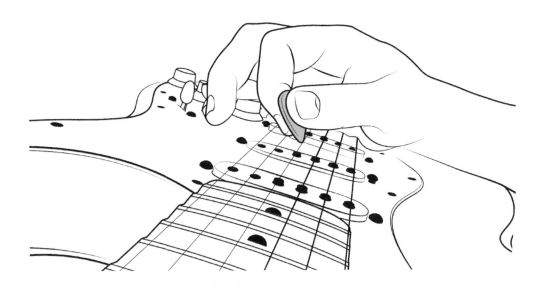

OK, it's time to dive in and learn to strum accurately, starting with one of the simplest things you can do when you're strumming: playing one chord per bar.

1. Begin by holding down an E Minor chord and play the exercise in Example 1a

2. Set your metronome to click at 60 beats per minute (bpm)

3. Before you play anything, count aloud along with the metronome "1 2 3 4 1 2 3 4" etc

4. Tap your foot on each metronome click (beat of the bar)

5. When counting and tapping your foot feel natural together, you're ready to play your chord

6. Use a down strum to play the E Minor chord on the first beat of each bar (every time you say "one")

7. After you have played the chord, raise your strumming hand back up, to reset and repeat the strum the next time you say "one" out loud. Your hand should move up with your foot and wait while you count "two, three, four"

Strum the chord every time you get back to beat one. Notice your foot. Has it shifted out of time? Are you still able to count out loud?

In American English, a note that lasts for a whole bar (measure) is called a *whole note*. In The UK it's called a *semibreve*.

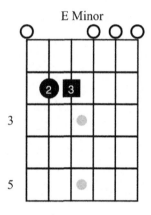

E Minor

Example 1a:

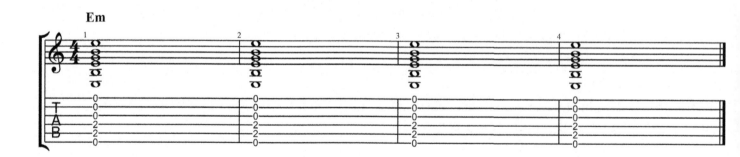

When you can play along comfortably with the audio track, move on and try Example 1b.

This time, you're going to strum on beat one *and* beat three.

Repeat steps 1-5 above before you stum the E Minor with a down stroke on both beat one and beat three.

Again, pay attention to your foot and your voice. Are you still tapping on the beat and able to count out loud?

In North America, a note that lasts half a bar is called a *half note*. In the UK it's called a *minim*.

Example 1b:

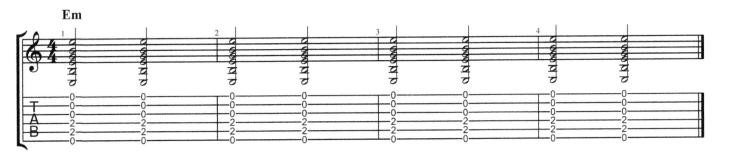

Let's double up. In the follow exercise, I want you to play a down strum on every single beat of the bar. Set yourself up using steps 1-5 again, then strum the Em chord on beats 1, 2, 3 and 4.

Your foot and strumming hand should be moving together. As your foot goes down, so should your strumming hand. After you've played the E Minor chord, your hand should lift back up in sync with your foot.

These rhythms are called *1/4 notes* (or *crotchets* in the UK). 1/4 notes look like this and are played by strumming *Down, Down, Down, Down.*

Look at the notation part above the tablature. You'll see these rhythms written out along with the notes of the chord.

Example 1c:

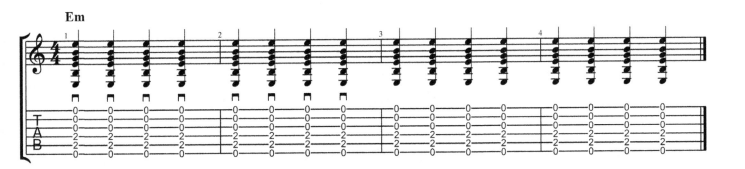

Let's introduce the next subdivision, *1/8th notes* (*quavers* in the UK).

As you might have guessed, a bar of music contains eight 1/8th notes and to play them we need to use an *up strum*. In the previous example, we used four down strokes to play four 1/4 notes in each bar.

To play 1/8th notes, all we need to do is add an up strum between each of the down strums. Instead of "Down, Down, Down, Down", we will play "Down-Up, Down-Up, Down-Up, Down-Up".

The easiest way to learn this is to play one measure of 1/4 notes followed by one measure of 1/8th notes. All you need to do is squeeze an up strum in between each down strum.

On paper, 1/8th notes look like this. Notice that the down strokes are all still in the same place on the beat, we're just squeezing in an extra up stroke between each one.

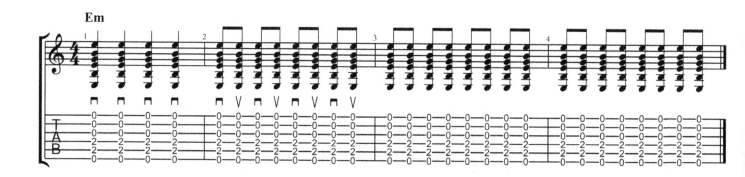

Repeat steps 1-5 to get you ready to play the next example, then play along with the audio. Keep your foot tapping and focus on keeping each down-up strum even – both rhythmically and in volume.

Do your usual checks to make sure you're still tapping in time. As your foot goes down, you'll be playing the down strum, as your foot comes up you'll be playing the up strum.

It will help if you count out loud "one *and* two *and* three *and* four *and*" with the "ands" coinciding with the up strums.

Look to see how the down and up strums are notated. A down strum is marked with a ⊓ and up strum is marked with a ∨. (Yes! I know the notation for up strum looks like a down arrow!).

Example 1d:

Now, we could keep going and splitting each rhythm in half. After 1/8th notes, we can play 1/16th notes, 1/32nd notes, and even 1/64th notes. However, if you're playing rock, pop or blues, you'll find that most rhythms used are based around 1/4 notes and 1/8th notes, so it makes sense to focus the majority of your time on these beat divisions before moving on to more intricate ideas.

1/16th notes are often used in hard rock, metal and funk, and as you might imagine, there are lots of permutations of how they can be arranged. For now, let's build your strumming technique by learning to perfectly combine the rhythms we've covered so far.

For the following examples, use the steps we've covered to set yourself up before playing anything. Your foot should be tapping along with the click and you should be counting out loud. Throughout, keep your focus on your foot. If it moves out of time and isn't perfectly syncing with the beat, stop, take a minute and try the exercise again.

These examples are played with an A Minor chord, but feel free to use other chords if you get bored. We'll learn how to change chords in time later.

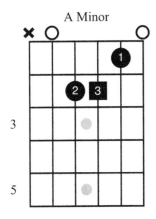

In Example 1e, combine a 1/2 note with two 1/4 notes. As this is an Am chord, ensure you strum it from the 5th string and don't play the 6th string (the low E).

Example 1e:

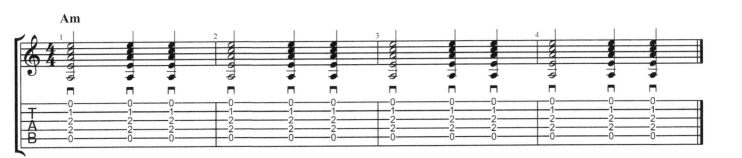

This time, play 1/4 notes on beats 1, 2 and 4 and play 1/8th notes on beat 3. The strumming pattern is Down, Down, Down-Up, Down.

Look at the notation line above the tablature and see what these rhythms look like when written. Learning to read rhythm is a valuable skill and understanding these rhythms is important for what will come later in the book.

Example 1f:

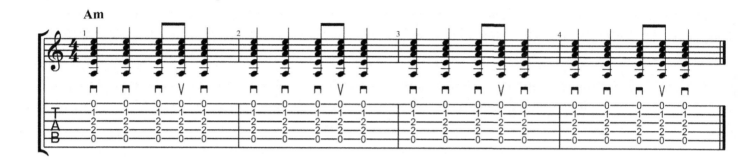

Now try Down, Down-Up, Down-Up, Down.

Example 1g:

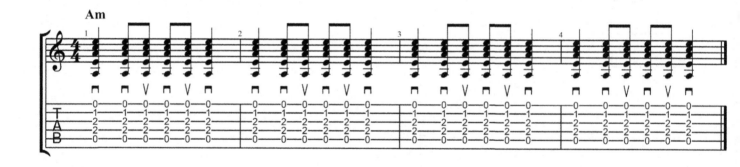

This time play Down, Down, Down-Up, Down.

Example 1h:

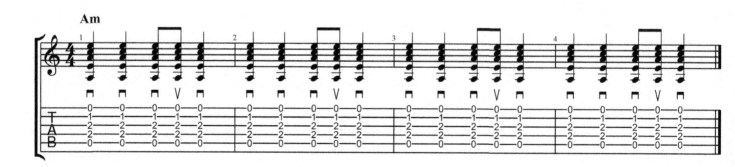

The next example is a bit more involved as the strumming pattern lasts for two bars.

In the first bar play Down, Down, Down-Up, Down.

In the second bar play Down-Up, Down-Up, Down, Down.

It's very common for music to contain strumming patterns that repeat every two, or even every four bars. Listen to your favourite tracks and focus your ears on the strumming patterns. Listen to the placement of the chords and count along with the music to see how long it takes for the rhythm pattern to repeat.

Example 1i:

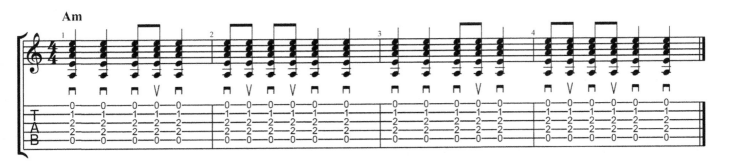

Here are some more two-bar phrases. Once you've mastered the patterns, try playing different chords in each bar. For example, you could play E Minor in bar one and A Minor in bar two. However, right now it's more important for you to master the rhythm than to worry about changing chords. There'll be plenty of time for that later. Get your rhythms tight and the chord changes will follow more easily.

This two-bar rhythm is played:

Bar one: Down, Down, Down (hold)

Bar two: Down, Down, Down-Up, Down-Up

Example 1j:

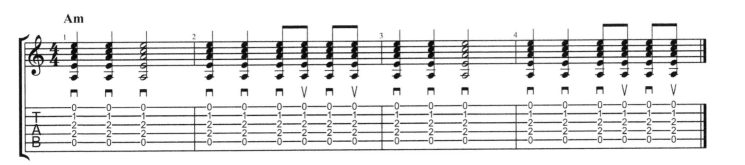

Try this pattern.

Bar one: Down-Up, Down-Up, Down, Down

Bar two: Down-Up, Down, Down-Up, Down

Example 1k:

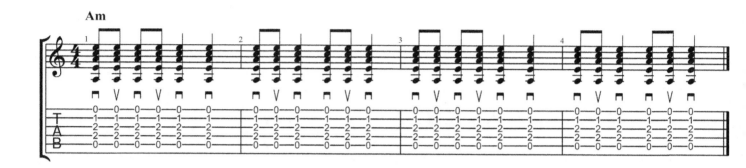

Here's a two-bar rhythm that builds in intensity.

Bar one: Down, Down

Bar two: Down, Down, Down-Up, Down-Up

Example 1l:

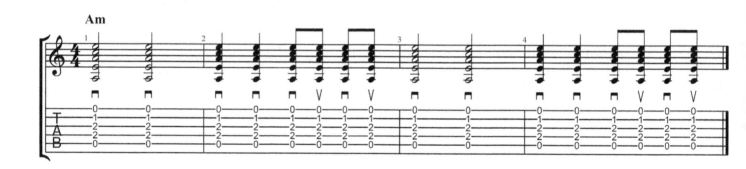

Let's build up your stumming stamina! Here are a few four-bar rhythms that are created by combining the rhythms from some of the previous two-bar examples.

Bar one: Down-Up, Down-Up, Down Down

Bar two: Down-Up, Down, Down-Up Down

Bar three: Down, Down

Bar four; Down, Down, Down-Up, Down-Up

Example 1m:

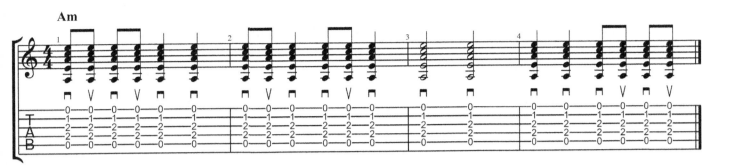

Bar one: Down, Down, Down-Up, Down

Bar two: Down-Up, Down-Up, Down Down

Bar three: Down-Up, Down-Up, Down, Down

Bar four: Down-Up, Down, Down-Up, Down

Example 1n:

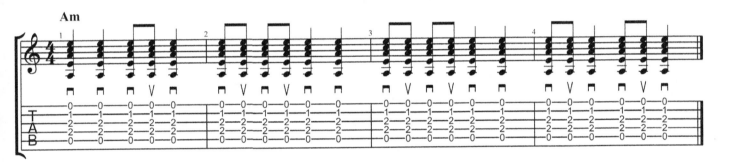

In this chapter we've covered a lot of ideas.

We began with the idea that your foot should always be tapping and that your strumming hand always moves in the same direction as your foot, to lock in the rhythm physically with your body.

We broke down the basic rhythms of music and converted them into specific strumming patterns.

We combined these rhythms into more interesting musical ideas and added chords.

We also looked at longer rhythms that lasted for two and four bars. These ideas are the patterns you'll find in a great many pop and rock tracks.

I want to round off this chapter by suggesting a few chord combinations you can use with these examples. Go slow and use your metronome. The priority is to get the strumming patterns correct, even if the chords don't always land cleanly. Even if you make a mistake in your fretting hand, learn to keep your strumming hand moving accurately. Whatever you do, don't stop. If you make a mistake on stage, you can't stop in the middle of a song to correct yourself. It's important that you learn to stay in time and make sure you get the next chord right! Your audience will notice a bad rhythm before they notice a bad note.

Go back through the chapter and try using the following chord combinations. For the one-bar examples, change chords each time you repeat the pattern.

Chord Combinations

1.

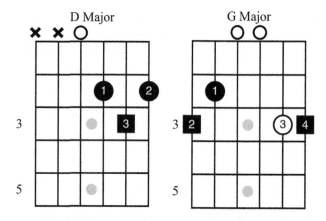

2.

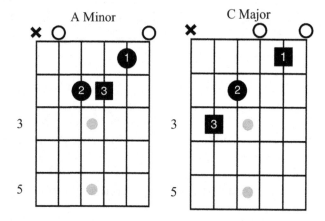

3.

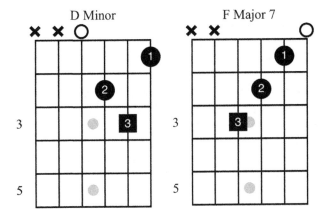

4.

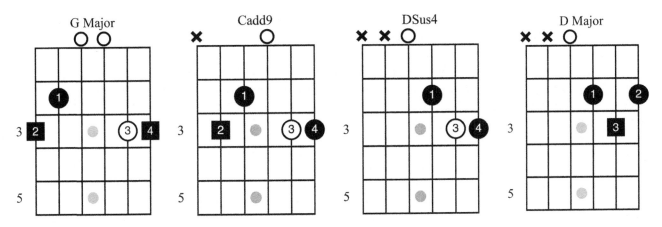

In the next chapter we're going to make these strumming patterns a bit cooler and by learning how to push and pull the rhythms using a technique called *syncopation*.

Chapter Two: Pushing and Pulling

Most music doesn't stick to just playing chords directly on the beats. Often, the chords fall between the beats to create more energy and groove. The proper term for this idea is *syncopation*.

The simplest and most common way to add energy to your rhythm playing is to *miss out* strumming some down beats. To teach you this idea, we need to introduce a new musical symbol. It is an 1/8th note *rest* and it looks like this: 𝄾

This rest simply means *silence* or "don't strum". It will always be seen in combination with a strummed 1/4 note so that together they add up to *one beat*, like this: 𝄾 ♪

Before, when we played the rhythm ♫ the strumming pattern was Down-Up.

With the rhythm 𝄾 ♪ we *miss out the down strum* but *still play the up strum.*

To make this easier, it's important to always keep moving the strumming hand as if you are going to play the down strum, but simply *miss the strings*. This will keep you in time.

In other words, the strumming hand is going up and down constantly, but *does not make contact* with the strings on the down strum. This is shown in the notation below by placing brackets around the arrow.

To practice this idea, study the following rhythm:

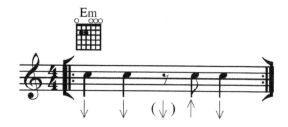

Count out loud: "Down, Down, *Miss*-Up, Down

To play the rhythm, keep the strumming hand moving all the time. Play down strokes on the first two beats of the bar. Miss the strings on the down strum of beat 3, but make contact on the following up strum before playing the down strum on beat 4.

This example is written out over two bars below. Listen carefully to the audio and play along. Tap your foot on the beat.

You'll get the most out of the following examples if you loop them for a few minutes. It'll help the strumming movements become more natural.

Example 2a:

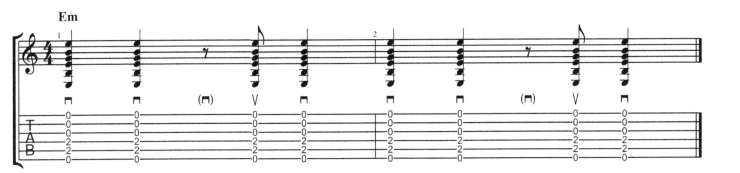

The following example is played with a D Major chord and misses the down strum of beat two. Pay attention to the notation part and look out for the rests. It's played, Down, *Miss*-Up, Down, Down.

Example 2b:

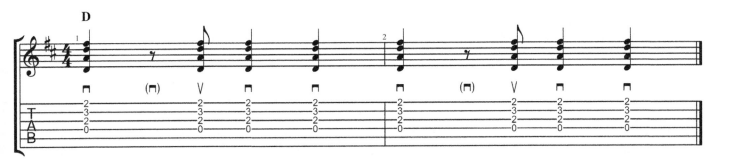

This example misses the up strum on beats two and three. Play, Down, *Miss*-Up, *Miss*-Up, Down.

Example 2c:

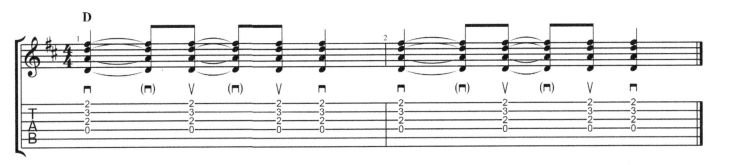

This idea misses out the whole of beat 2 using a 1/4 note rest, and the down strum of beat 4. Play this one as Down, *Rest*, Down, *Miss*-Up

Remember to keep your strumming hand moving during the rest on beat 2.

Keep looping this example until it becomes comfortable and natural.

Example 2d:

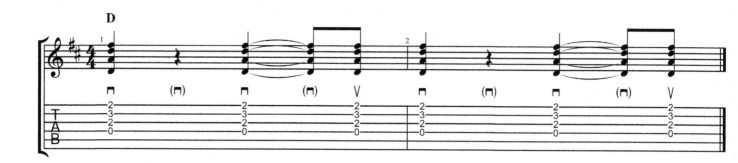

Let's keep going and explore some more possibilities. I know this may seem a little formulaic, but I promise I'm going somewhere musical with all of this!

In Example 2e you're going to only play a downstroke on beat one. All the strums are on the *up beat*.

Example 2e:

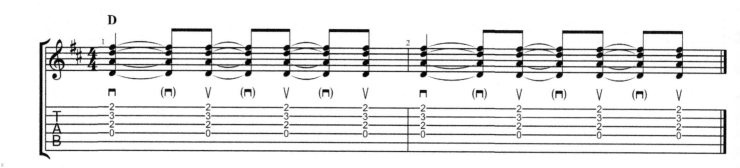

Here's the biggest challenge so far. Now all the up beats are played, but none of the down beats. The secret to playing rhythms like this accurately is to set yourself up properly during the count in.

Make sure you're tapping your foot and moving your hand up and down as you count in with the audio track. Say out loud, "*Miss*-Up, *Miss*-Up, *Miss*-Up, *Miss*-Up" as your hand moves over the strings.

Continue this movement when it's time to play. Miss the strings with the first down strum and connect with the strings on the up strum. Repeat this movement four times and you'll have played the entire bar.

It's important that you keep checking in with your body. Are you still tapping your foot on the beat? These physical movements are the key to *internalising* the rhythms. You don't want to have to *think* about the rhythms you're playing. You need to learn to *feel* them in relation to the beat.

Play Example 2f with a D Major chord.

Example 2f:

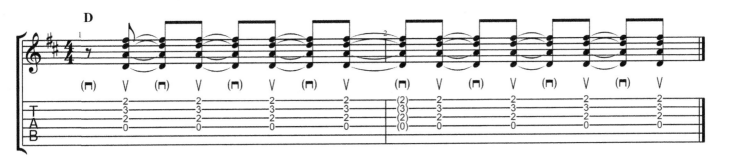

Let's look at some two-bar stumming patterns made up from the rhythms we have covered so far. The patterns are different in bars one and two. Use whichever chords you like for the examples, and if you can change chords between bars one and two, all the better. However, for now it's more important to focus on your stumming hand and build the muscle memory there, before thinking too much about building chord sequences. We will get to that later though!

Break down the following examples and learn the patterns for each bar individually before putting them together.

I've written the following examples with an E Minor in bar one and an A Minor in bar two. You can ignore this and play one chord throughout when you're just starting out. When you get more confident, play the chords as written, and if you're feeling pretty good, try adding your own chords.

The two-bar pattern can be broken down as,

Bar one: Down, Down Up, *Miss*-Up, Down

Bar two: Down-Up, Down-Up, Down, Down

Example 2g:

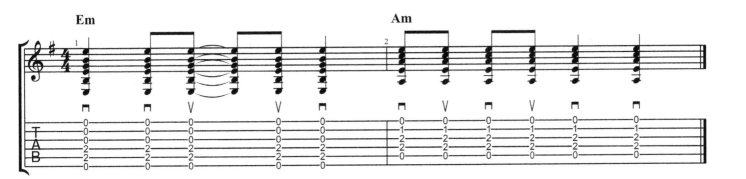

The following idea is played,

Bar one: Down-Up, *Miss*-Up, *Miss*-Up, Down

Bar two: Down-Up, *Miss*-Up, Down, *Rest*

Example 2h:

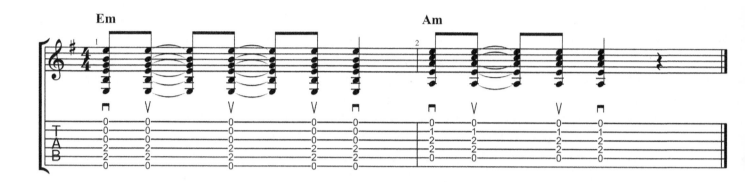

This one is harder as there's no down strum on beat 1. Count in properly and tap your foot.

Bar 1: *Miss*-Up, *Miss*-Up, *Miss*-Up, Down

Bar 2: Down-Up, Down-Up, Down-Up, Down

Example 2i:

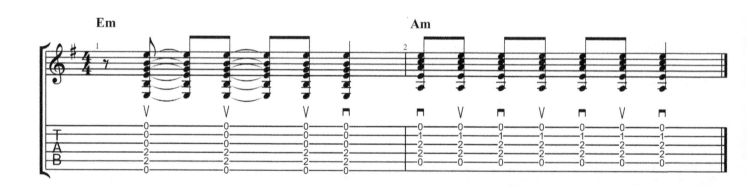

This example gets more syncopated as you move through the bars.

Bar 1: Down, Down, Down-Up, *Miss*-Up,

Bar 1: *Rest*-Up, *Miss*-Up, *Miss*-Up, Down

Example 2j:

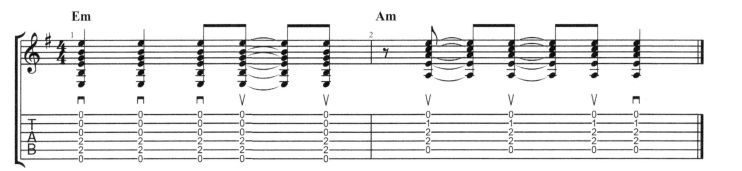

Here's an extremely common rhythm that's used in pop music all the time.

Bar 1: Down, *Miss*-Up, *Miss*-Up, Down

Bar 2: Down, *Miss*-Up, *Miss*-Up, Down-Up

Example 2k:

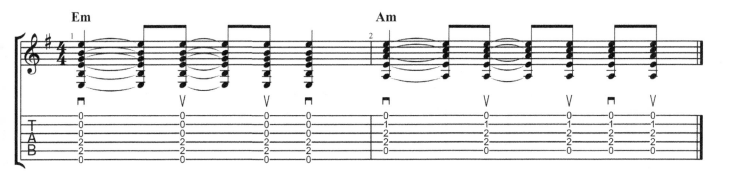

Work through the previous examples until they're rock solid and try introducing your own chords. You can apply these strumming patterns to any chord sequences you know.

The next concept to introduce is the idea of a *tied* rhythm. When two chords are tied together, you strum the first one as normal, then *hold* it for the value of the second one. You do not play the chord a second time, you just let the first chord ring out.

On paper, a tie is just written as a curved line and is often seen at the end of a bar tying two chords together *across the bar line*.

Take a look at the example below.

The first bar begins with a simple Down, Down, Down, on beats 1, 2 and 3. On beat 4 you will play a Down-Up strum.

Notice that the final 1/8th note of bar one is tied to the first 1/4 note of bar two. This means that you *do not* play the strum on beat 1 of bar two, you simply let the previous up strum ring until beat 2, where you continue with the down strums for the rest of the bar.

Play Example 2l with an A Minor chord throughout and listen carefully to the audio before learning the example with a click then playing along when you're confident.

Example 2l:

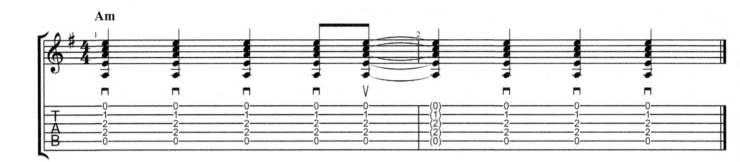

Now try this idea. It's similar but this time the final 1/8th note is tied to the first 1/8th note of bar two. The first strum you play in bar two is the up stroke on the "and" of beat 1.

Example 2m:

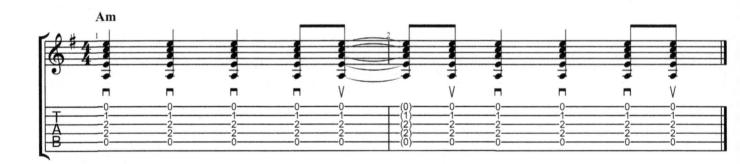

Here's one more example to help you master this feel. The final up stroke on beat 4 is again tied to the first 1/8th of bar two, but this time the 1/8th note rest on beat 4 makes the rhythm a little more challenging. Pay careful attention to the audio track and learn this one very carefully. Keep your foot tapping!

Example 2n:

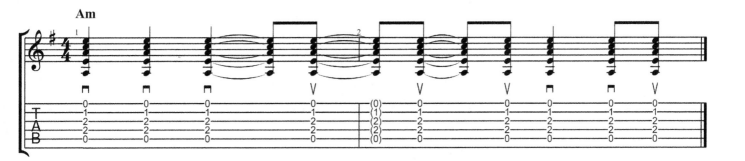

Ties (and rests) are very useful because one thing they can do is teach us to change chord slightly before or after the bar. For example, instead of changing chord on beat 1 of bar two, you could change chord on the "and" (up strum) of beat 4. This creates the effect of "pushing" the music forward and adds a bit of energy. Of course, it's not always appropriate to do this, so listen carefully to the track you're learning before playing with the rhythm too much.

Let's learn how to push a chord change an 1/8th note before the bar line.

This example uses the chords A Major and D Major. If you can, play the A Major as a one-finger barre chord and focus on only hitting the 5th, 4th, 3rd and 2nd strings. If you want to play it the conventional way with three fingers, that's fine too.

Hold down A Major and play down strums on the first three beats of the bar, then a *Miss*-Up on beat 4. The catch is that you need to change to D Major on the up strum just before the start of bar two! If this is too quick, try the exercise with easier chords like E Minor and A Minor.

Notice that the D Major chord on beat "4 and" is tied to the 1/4 note on beat 1 and the next strum you'll play is the down stroke on beat 2. Fill out the rest of bar 2 with 1/4 note strums.

Example 2o:

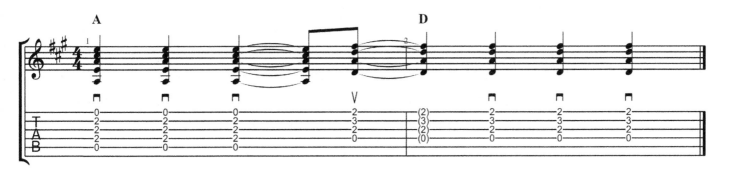

Here's a similar example that uses the same push to D Major on beat 4 of bar one. This time, however, the rhythm in bar two is a bit more interesting and adds movement to the chord sequence.

Listen carefully to the audio before you play this idea. Keep your strumming moving up and down with the beat at all times and, as always, tap your foot.

Example 2p:

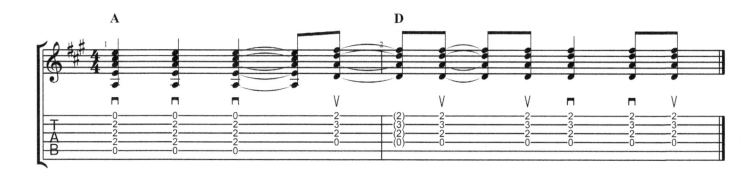

Here's another idea using the same push to D on beat "4 and", but now I've added some movement to bar one.

Example 2q:

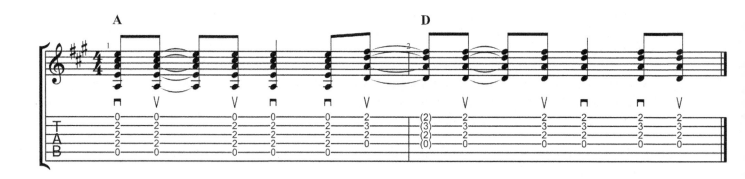

In the next example, you're going to push the chord at beginning of bar one *and* the beginning of bar two.

This means that the first chord of bar one is played on beat "4 and" of the count in.

To learn to play this, listen carefully to the audio. Count out loud along with the click saying, "one and two and three and four and". Tap your foot and move your strumming hand up and down in time with the beat.

You'll quickly notice and hear that the first A Major chord is played with an up strum just before beat 1 of the first bar. I've kept the other rhythms simple throughout each bar but look out for the similar push onto the D Major chord at the end of bar one.

Example 2r:

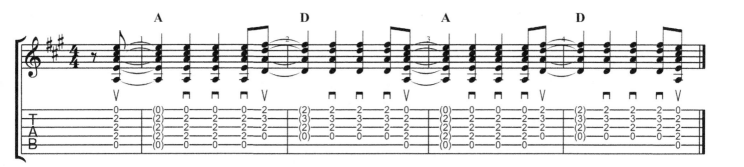

Now try filling out the strumming pattern a little bit in each bar. Listen to the audio before attempting this example.

Example 2s:

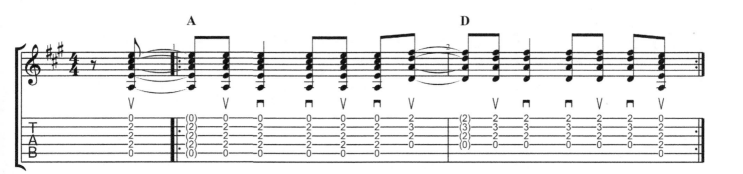

I think you're starting to get the idea!

Have fun making up your own syncopated rhythms and try them out with different combinations of chords. Spend time listening to your favourite tunes and see if you can hear how the guitar rhythm locks in with, or cuts across, the drums and bass.

In the next chapter we'll spend time making this all a bit more musical.

Chapter Three: Acoustic Pop Strumming Patterns

In this chapter I'm going to move away from the nuts and bolts of strumming and simply give you ten chord sequences that underpin a lot of the pop music you'll hear today. I've written a different chord sequence for each example to help inspire a bit of songwriting on your part.

Each sequence comes with a suggested strumming pattern, but you don't have to use this pattern. You can feel free to chop and change strumming patterns, based on what you've already learnt, and also change up the chords, speed and energy if you want.

I've written most of the chord sequences as four-bar progressions, but the strumming pattens may repeat every one, two or four bars. Once you can play each example, loop it for a while and see if it speaks to you.

As always, have a careful listen to the audio track before attempting each example, and remember to tap your foot on the beat.

Example 3a:

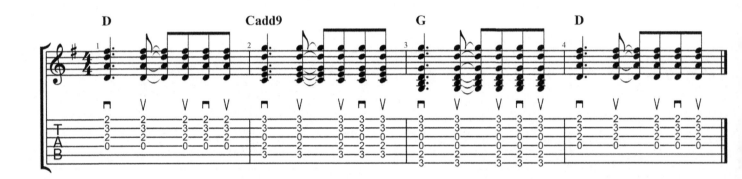

Example 3b:

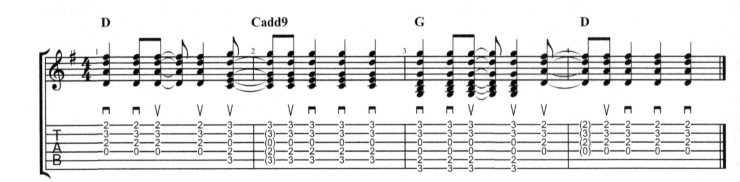

Example 3c:

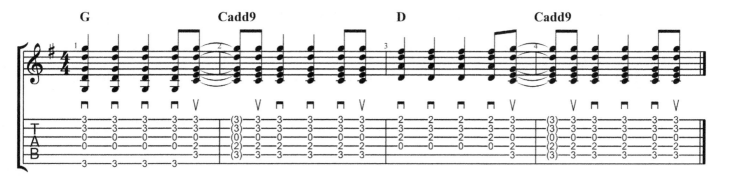

Example 3d:

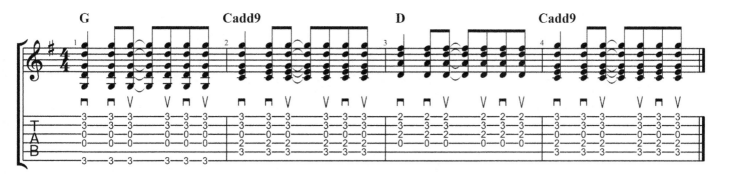

Example 3e:

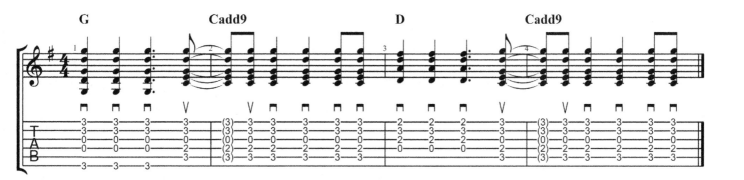

Example 3f:

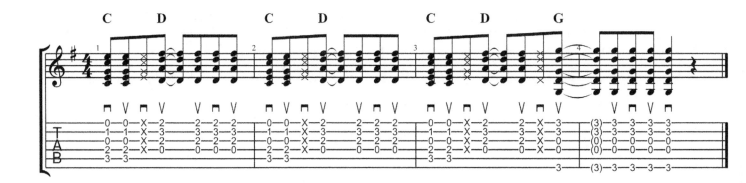

Example 3g:

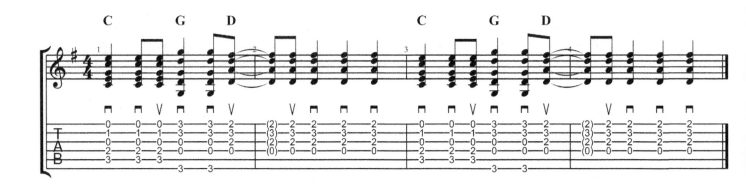

Example 3h:

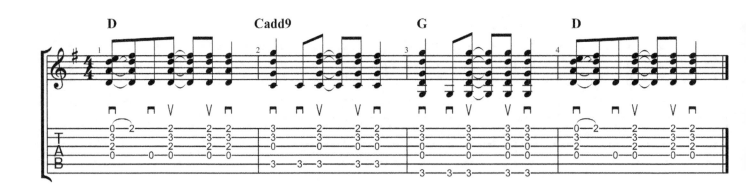

Example 3i:

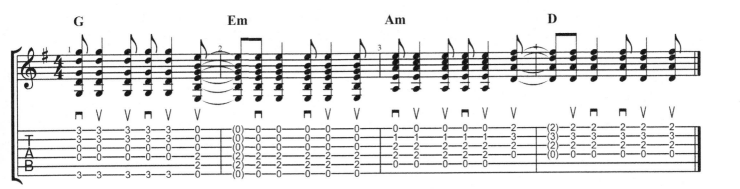

Example 3j:

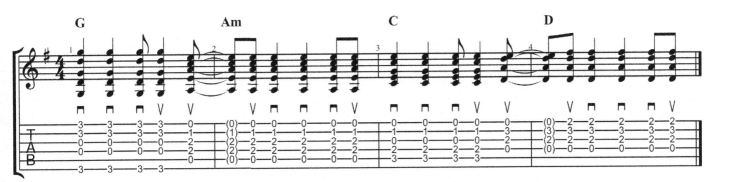

OK, so you now have a collection of effective strumming patterns under your fingers, and also some popular chord sequences that crop up in all sorts of music.

Next, you're going to learn how to break the "rules" of strumming and play some new rock guitar ideas that only use down strokes.

Chapter Four: Down Strum Rock Patterns

As a teacher, it's always lovely to be able to give a student a consistent set of rules to follow that will work every time. And, to be fair, the rule of *strum down on a down beat* and *up on an up beat* will pretty much always work perfectly. However, music is always a bit more subtle than arbitrary rules, and sometimes we need to break those rules if we want to create a particular *sound*. After all, music is all about sounds and feelings, right?

So, take a moment to think about the difference in the sound created by a down strum and an up strum. When you play a down strum, you hit the bass strings first and bring out most of the low end of the chord. When you play an up strum it's the opposite. You hit the high-pitched strings first and bring out more of the treble in the chord.

When you're playing big acoustic style strummed chords, this creates a lot of beautiful contrasting textures that work well in that context, but what if you are playing something a bit darker, like rock or heavy metal? Maybe you don't want to introduce all those rich textures. Maybe you just want to create a more uniform sound.

For this reason, it's not uncommon to play every chord with a down strum, and this is particularly true for the type of power chord rock we'll look at in this section.

Now, I do want to take a moment to say that whether you use down strums exclusively or stick with a more natural down and up strum pattern, it's entirely your choice. What I will advise you to do is work through this entire chapter twice. The first time, play the exercises as written using only down strums. Then, when you've got the feel for that, repeat the chapter using the more standard down and up strums you learnt in the previous sections.

The most important thing is to listen to the sound you're making on the guitar. Try plugging in and adding a little bit of overdrive to your tone. Does this make a difference to how you feel about the music you're making?

All of these things are artistic choices you can control, and the best way to understand the effect your approach has is to try many different ones.

With all of that out of the way, let's quickly take a look at *power chords* – the type of chords you're going to be using in this chapter.

The chords we've used so far are all fairly rich sounding, but power chords strip back the harmony to just two notes. There are two main ways to play them. The first is with just two notes:

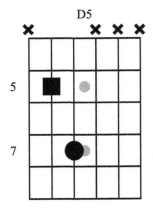

And the second is with three notes.

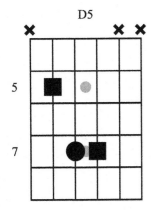

The second chord is a bit brighter than the first and again, it's a musical choice as to which one you use. In the following examples I'll write them with two notes but feel free to use the three-note version. Both of these chords are named D5.

Let's dive in and start playing these chords with down stroke strumming patterns. Heads up! This might feel a little weird after the first few chapters but stick with it! This is an important technique to know.

We'll start with an easy one. Hold down a D5 chord and play 1/4 notes with down strums. For now, let each chord ring.

Example 4a

Now let's add in 1/8th notes on beat 3. It might feel counterintuitive at first, but you're going to play the 1/8th notes with down strums. There are no up strums in these exercises!

Example 4b:

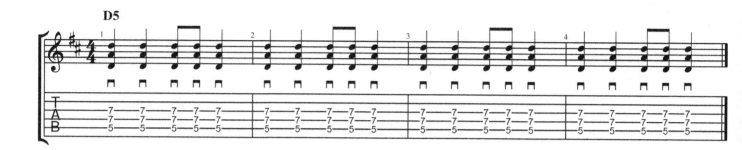

This time play 1/8th notes on beats 2 and 4.

Example 4c:

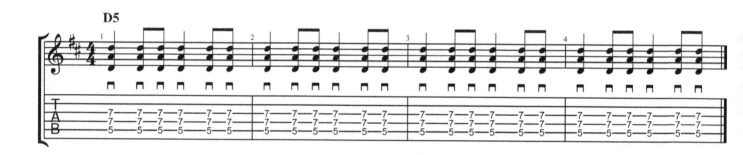

Now I want to introduce you to a new technique called *palm muting*.

If you've not come across palm muting before it's a way to slightly deaden the strings using the "karate chop" part of your strumming hand.

The simplest way to describe this is that you rest the fleshy part of the underside of your strumming hand very gently on the strings you're going to be playing. You can move your hand forwards and backwards along the strings slightly to cause more or less muting.

For example, if your hand is so far back it's touching the bridge of the guitar, you'll still get some of the harmonics of the chord ringing through. If you move it forward towards the first pickup (or sound hole on an acoustic guitar) you'll mute more.

The placement of your hand is about trial and error, so listen to the following example as I play two strums with no muting, then palm mute to varying degrees to create a less or more dampened effect.

Example 4d:

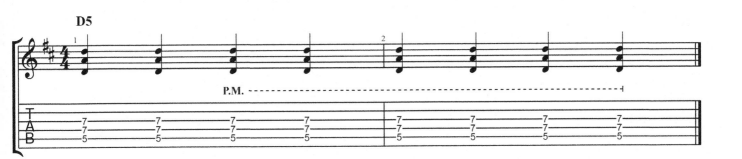

Play the next example a few times using different amounts of muting and all down strokes. Add some overdrive and see how aggressive you can make it sound. Make sure that the notes don't ring out and you keep the middle two beats silent by muting with your palm. It just goes to show that a bit of muting and some space create a powerful riff – even with just one chord.

Example 4e:

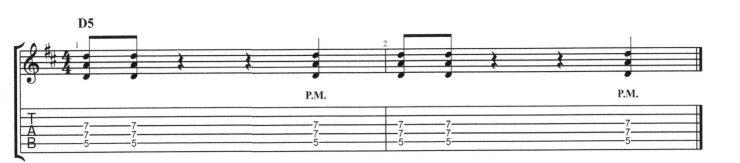

The most difficult thing for most students to do it to learn to play up rhythms with down strokes. After all, you're used to playing up beats with up strokes! And, as you've seen, playing up strokes on up beats feels natural as the movement of your hand matches the movement of your foot.

To learn to play a down stroke on a syncopated up beat rhythm, try the following D5 example. It's similar to the previous idea, but the final strum in the bar is delayed by an 1/8th note to place it on the "4 and" of the bar. At first, you'll probably find that placing the strum accurately is a bit of a challenge. It's definitely a case of mind over matter!

Listen to the audio first and play along once you can play the exercise with your metronome.

Example 4f:

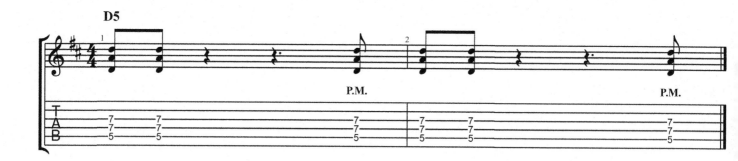

When that starts to feel comfortable, try the next two exercises.

Example 4g:

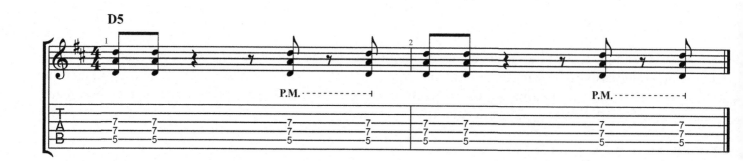

Example 4h:

OK, now you're getting the feel for using only down strokes, learn these two two-bar patterns. Experiment with muting and try moving the power chord around too!

Example 4i:

Try muting all but the final two notes in this example.

Example 4j:

Let's play the same rhythm again but this time move from a muted D5 down two frets to a C5 in bar two.

Example 4k:

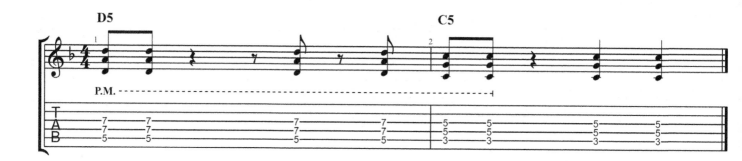

Before we move on to playing these rhythms with some cool chord sequences, try playing the next example that pushes the chord change to C5 on to the "4 and" of bar one, just like you learned in Chapter Two. Let the first strum of the C5 ring out to emphasis the change. Listen to the audio if you get stuck.

Example 4l:

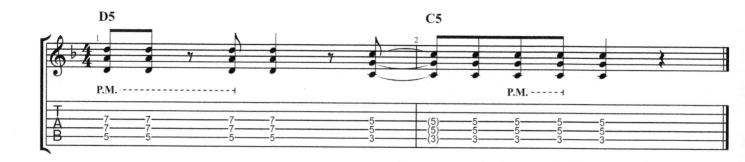

This example uses a tie in the middle of bar one as well as at the end. Let the tied chords ring and mute the others.

Example 4m:

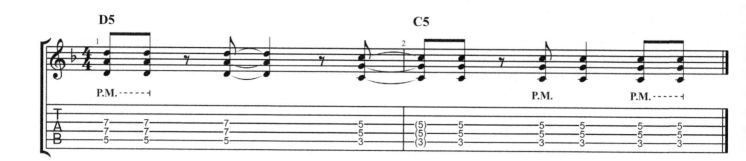

To round off this chapter, here are ten power chord sequences that use different strumming patterns. The rhythm patterns can be one, two, or four bars long, but each one uses a new chord sequence to help inspire your creativity.

Notice that you sometimes change chords in the middle of the bar, and that some chord changes are pushed while others are not.

As I mentioned at the top of the chapter. Play all these examples using down strokes, then try them again using the down up strumming you learnt earlier. There are no rights or wrongs, just opportunities to create different sounds and feels.

Example 4n:

Example 4o:

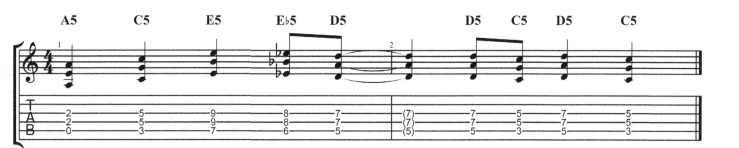

Example 4p:

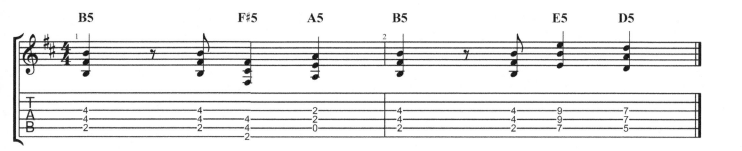

Example 4q:

Example 4r:

Example 4s:

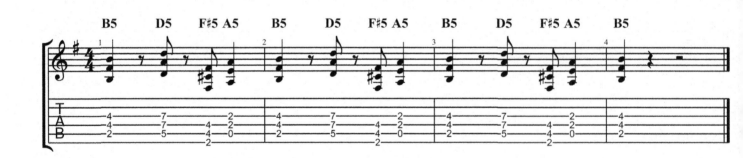

Example 4t:

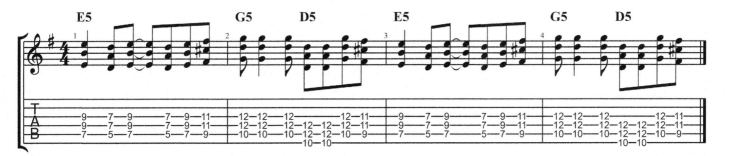

Example 4u:

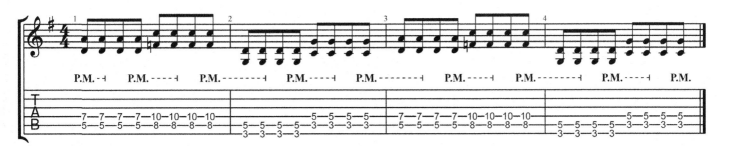

Example 4v:

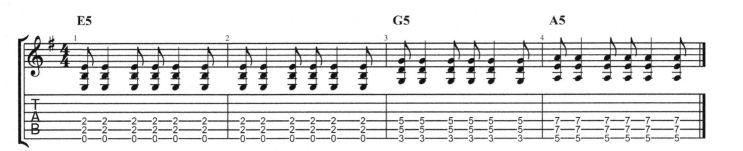

Example 4w:

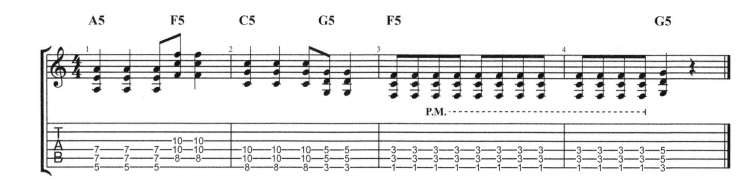

Chapter Five: 1/16th Note Rhythms

Now that you understand 1/8th note rhythms, we can start to explore the 1/16th note (semiquaver) divisions that are common in modern rock guitar. While 1/16th notes obviously occur in all types of music, you'll often find that hard rock, funk, rap and metal are actually built around 1/16th notes rhythms.

1/16th notes are created when we "double up" 1/8th notes. Instead of playing two divisions per beat, 1/16th notes split each beat into four to create sixteen subdivisions in each bar.

The most important thing you can do is learn to count 1/16th notes and play them in time with your tapping foot. Play the following exercise without a metronome at first, before setting it to click at about 50bpm.

Mute your strings with your strumming hand, so that when you strum the guitar you get a deadened *thwack* sound.

To divide each beat into four subdivisions, count out loud "*One* e and a *Two* e and a *Three* e and a *Four* e and a" and keep repeating this this while you strum the guitar down and up – one strum per syllable.

Your foot should be tapping every time you say a number, and this should coincide with the first down stroke on each beat. Strum, Down-Up Down-Up evenly, four strums per beat, and they should all sync up with your "one e and a" counting.

As you get more comfortable, try to make the first strum of every four slightly louder to accent the beat.

Example 5a

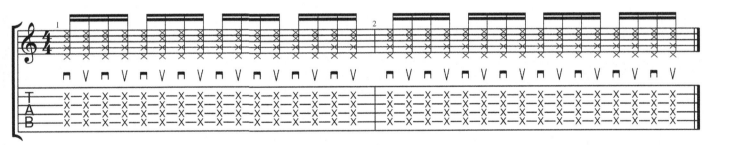

The next exercises teach you to move accurately between 1/4 notes, 1/8th notes and 1/16th notes.

Play Down strokes in bar one.

Play Down-Up strokes in bar two.

Double the speed of your Down-Up strokes in bar three.

Half the speed of your strokes in bar four.

Loop this exercise with your metronome set to 60bpm and listen carefully to your playing. Are you playing in time? Are your 1/16th notes evenly splitting the beat in four?

Record your playing on your phone and listen back. You might be surprised at what you hear.

Example 5b:

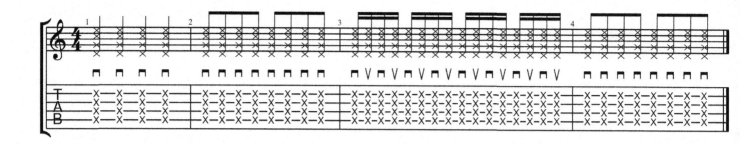

The next example combines 1/16th notes and 1/8th notes in one bar.

Example 5c

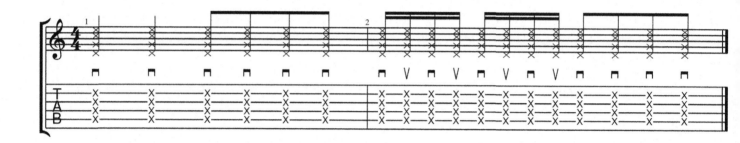

Try combining different rhythmic subdivisions and adding power chords to make the line musical.

Example 5d:

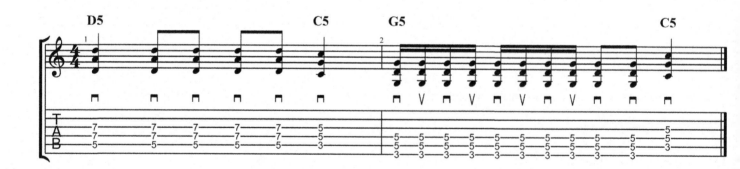

Example 5e:

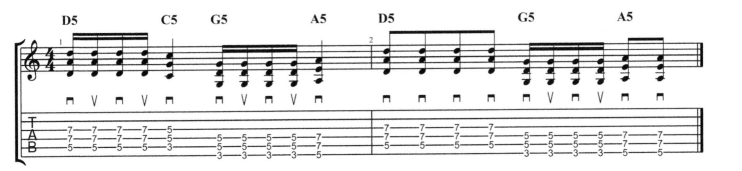

Let's move on and explore what happens when you start using ties to join 1/16th notes together.

Remember: a tie indicates that you *play* the first note and continue to *hold it* for the value of the second, tied note.

In the following example, I play continuous 1/16th notes for one bar, then tie together the first two 1/16th notes in each beat. My right hand does not stop moving up and down during the tied rhythm.

The following examples are notated using a single note for clarity in the diagrams. However, you should begin with fully muted strums as using a large movement will help you to be more accurate.

Example 5f:

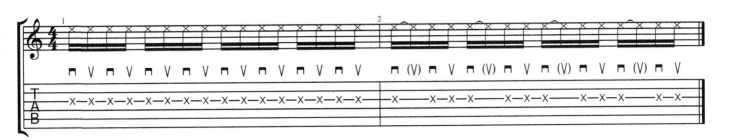

Listen to the audio and play through the exercise until you feel confident.

Tying together two 1/16th notes is mathematically the same as playing one 1/8th note (1/16 + 1/16 = 1/8).

This means that the previous example can be rewritten in the following way:

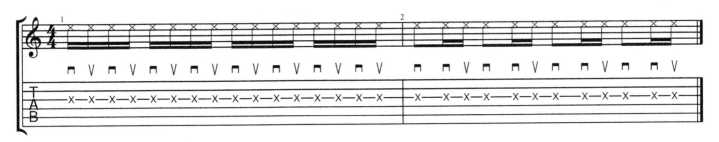

Although the previous two examples sound identical, you will probably find the second one easier to read. Notice that the picking/strumming pattern is identical.

By tying together different 1/16th notes we can create some of the most commonly used rhythms in music.

In the next example, the *middle* two 1/16th notes are tied together in the second bar. Remember to play these examples with fully muted strums across all the strings. Don't just play the single strings that are notated.

Example 5g:

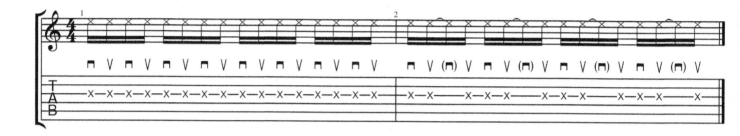

Again, the picking hand keeps moving Down-Up Down-Up but this time you miss out the second Down of each group: Down-Up *Miss*-Up, Down-Up *Miss*-Up

Here is the same diagram without the bracketed picks. You may find it clearer to read:

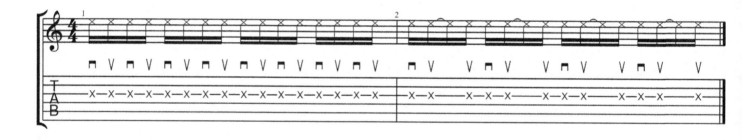

Applying the same logic as in Example 5a, this exercise can be rewritten as:

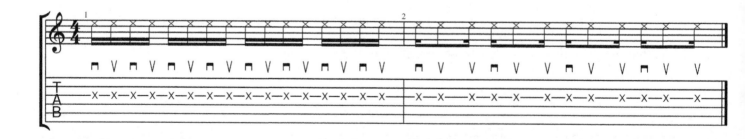

Play along with the audio track and make sure you tap your foot to the beat. It can be easy to get on the wrong side of these rhythms.

Finally (for now), tie together the final two 1/16th notes of each beat.

Example 5h:

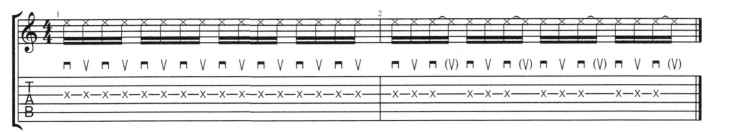

This can be written as:

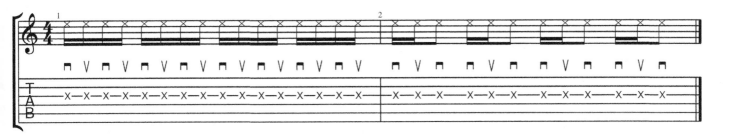

By tying together different pairs of 1/16th notes, we have created four different rhythmic groupings.

By combining these four 1/16th note rhythmic groupings, it is possible to create some extremely intricate rock guitar rhythms.

The combinations of these rhythms are virtually limitless, especially when you consider that we can also reintroduce rests to the phrases.

Before moving on, make sure you can play, recognise and read the four fundamental rhythmic building blocks of rock guitar shown in Example 5i.

Example 5i:

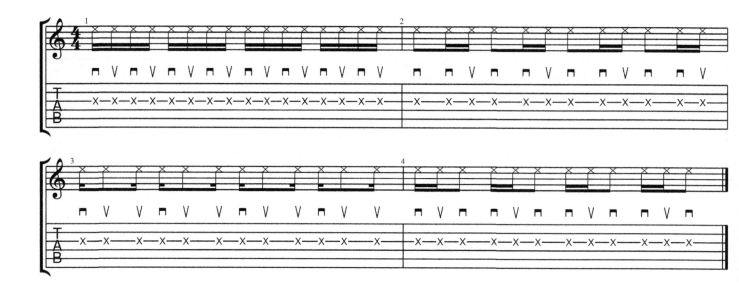

Play through Example 5i using fully muted strums before playing the exercise on a single muted string.

Now you have mastered the four main 1/16th note patterns, you can combine them into one-bar phrases. The following examples reintroduce power chords to make the rhythms musical and more interesting, although you may once again find it easier to start with muted strums as you master the rhythmic combinations.

Use palm muting to help you hear the rhythms more clearly.

Example 5j combines just two of the previous rhythms.

Example 5j:

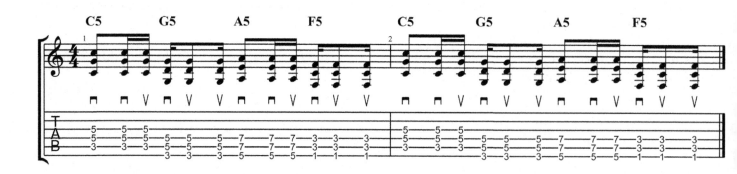

Example 5k combines three 1/16th note groupings.

Example 5k:

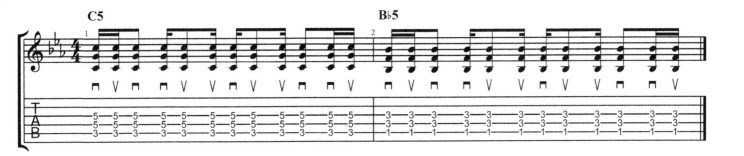

Example 5l uses the same three groupings in a different way.

Example 5l:

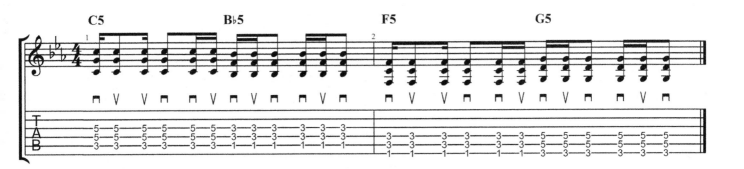

Example 5m uses all four 1/16th note groupings. Use heavy distortion and palm muting for a heavy metal vibe!

Example 5m:

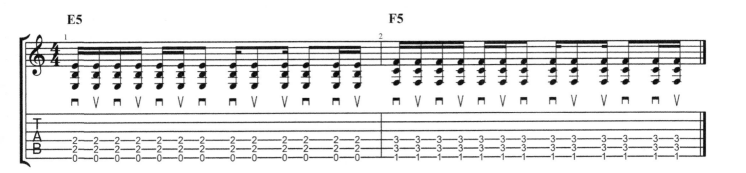

Example 5n shows another approach.

Example 5n:

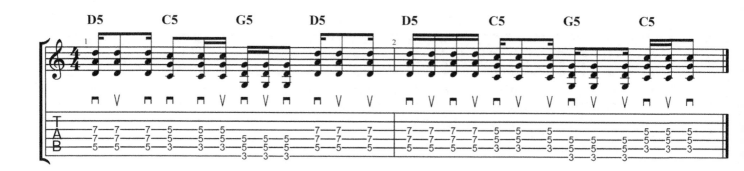

Finally, Example 5o reintroduces 1/8th note rests. You may find that the 1/8th note in beat 3 feels more natural as a down-strum.

Example 5o:

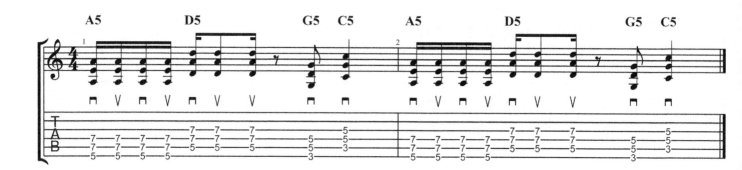

Make sure you're tapping your foot in time and that you emphasise the difference between the chords and the rests. This can be achieved by careful control of the pressure in the fretting hand.

Chapter Six: Rock Strumming Patterns with 1/16th Notes

After all the hard work in the previous chapter, I'm now going to teach you ten important rock strumming patterns that all use 1/16th notes in some way. Some will contain just a few, some will be quite busy. Each one is written with a cool chord sequence to help spur your creativity and can be a starting point for own songwriting.

The real secret is just to experiment and record yourself playing as often as possible. You'll quickly start coming up with your own ideas

Example 6a:

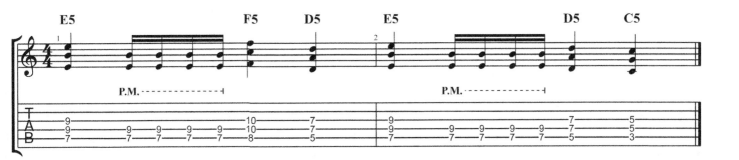

Example 6b:

Example 6c:

Example 6d:

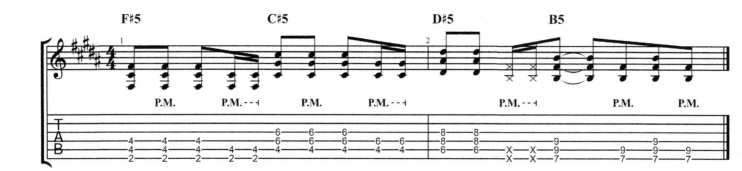

Example 6e:

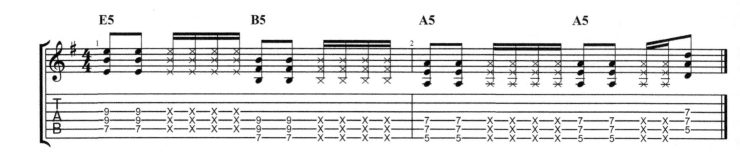

Example 6f:

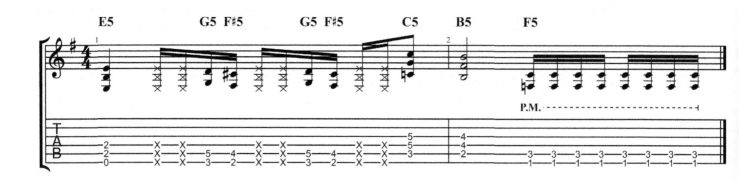

Example 6g:

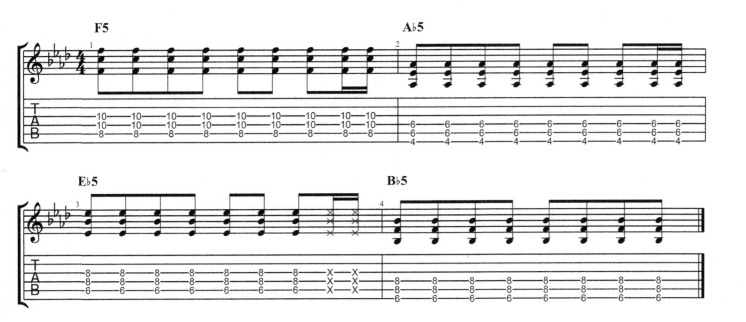

Example 6h:

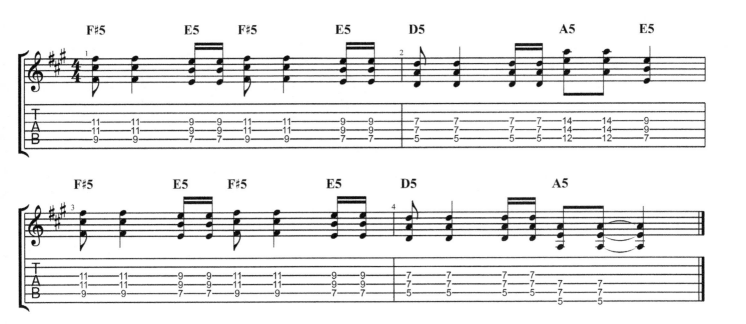

Example 6i:

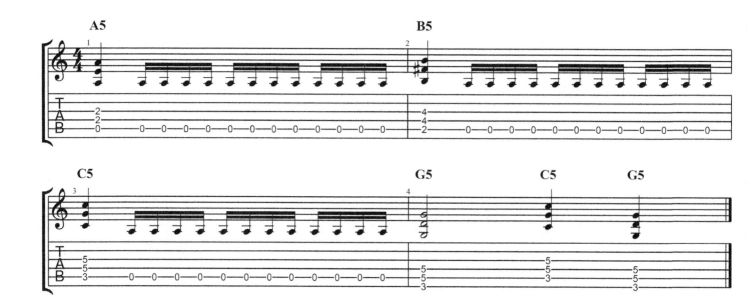

Example 6j:

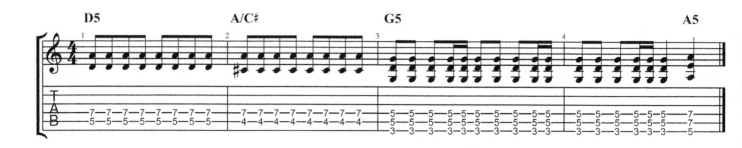

Chapter Seven: Funk 1/16th notes

It might come as a bit of a surprise, but since both genres are based around 1/16th notes, funk has a lot in common with rock when it comes to strumming patterns. Obviously, there is a different vibe to the music, but in terms of performance, they are similar in terms of their strumming patterns.

In funk music, it's normal to "embellish" rhythms by sliding into chords and I want to teach you that technique right now.

The first important funk rhythm guitar technique to learn is to *slide* a whole chord up the neck by a semitone. The idea is to start one semitone *below* the intended pitch, strike the chord, then slide the chord up to the target in one smooth movement.

Below is an E9 chord diagram. This is a common funk chord shape that has been used on countless hits from James Brown's *I Feel Good* onwards.

To target an E9 chord and embellish it with a side, I would strum an E♭9 (half a step down) and quickly slide the chord up a half step (one semitone) to the E9.

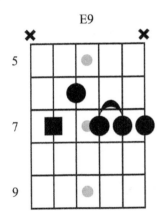

Rhythmically, there are three ways to approach this slide.

1) From the down beat to the off beat
2) From the off beat to the down beat
3) As a grace note (*appoggiatura*) where the slide is more "felt" than heard

Let's look at each of these ideas in turn.

In the first example, the Eb9 approach chord is played on the beat. It lasts for one 1/16th note and I arrive at the target E9 chord on the second 1/16th note of the bar.

These examples are easier to hear than to read, so make sure you listen to the audio tracks in this section.

Example 7a:

Pay careful attention to the strumming directions. Strum once on the Eb9, slide up a semitone and only strum again on beat two. Remember to strum harder than you think you need to! Here are a couple of examples that show this technique in context.

Example 7b uses an open sixth string on beat 1. Remember to keep your strumming hand moving up and down in constant 1/16th notes to help you stay in time.

In beat 2, perform the muted "scratch" notes by relaxing the pressure on the E9 chord but keep your fingers on the strings while you strum.

Example 7b:

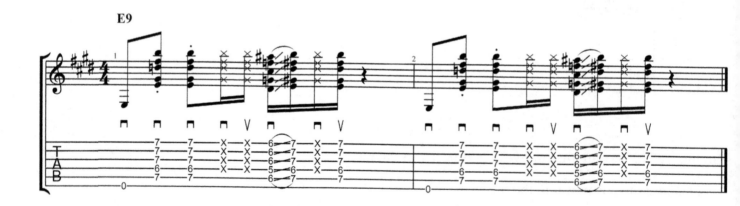

The next approach is to play the Eb9 chord on the final 1/16th note of the beat and slide it up so that the target chord is hit directly on the following down beat. This approach creates a very different rhythmic effect.

As the Eb9 chord is now on the fourth 1/16th note, it will be played with an upstroke.

Example 7c:

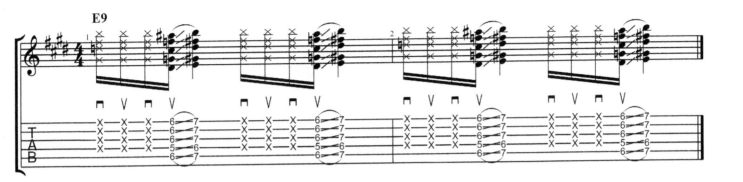

The following example demonstrates this technique used in a musical context. Notice the extra strum in bar two.

Example 7d:

This final approach is similar to the previous example where we move from the off beat to the down beat, however, this time the slide is much more subtle and less pronounced. The idea is to hit the target chord on the beat and give it a little *lead in* from below.

Example 7e:

The following two examples show some musical applications of the grace note slide.

Example 7f:

Example 7g:

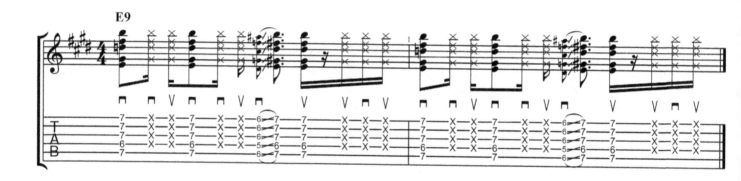

The E13 chord is closely related to the E9 chord and is very common in funk. It is formed by playing a standard E9 chord and simply reaching out with the little finger to play the 9th fret.

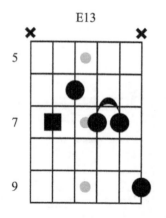

The following riff is written in the style of James Brown's guitarist Jimmy Nolen. You'll probably recognise it quickly. Play three E9 strums then use your little finger to reach for the E13 on beat 3.

It's common in funk to fill the gaps between the chord stabs with muted *scratched* strums, and you can see these occur at the end of beat 4. To perform them, leave your fretting fingers in contact with the strings but relax the pressure to create the iconic "thwack" sound.

Example 7h:

This example combines the scratched strums with an Eb9 to E9 slide on beat two. Reach out your little finger to reach the E13 on beat 3. Learn each beat separately before combining everything smoothly.

Example 7i:

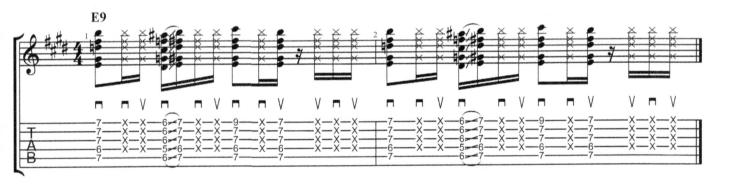

Here are a few other important funk guitar chords and voicings.

This minor 7 chord voicing with a root on the fifth string is essential to know.

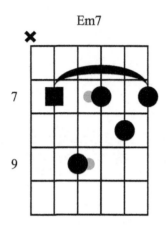

Once again, this is a movable barre chord form, so you can shift it up and down the neck into new keys.

To get familiar with this voicing, go through exercises 7a to 7i and replace the E9 chord with the Em7 chord voicing above.

You may be wondering how to alter the Em7 chord to accommodate the "13" voicing in Example 7h.

As with the E9 chord, there are similar alterations that can be made to the m7 voicing. These work in the same way as the E9 to E13 movement.

Simply add your little finger on the top string.

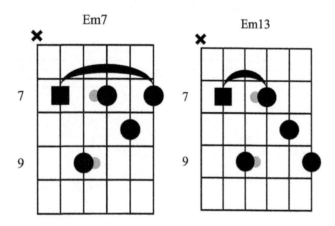

You can experiment with this note to get a crunchy minor sound in your rhythm work. Try moving from the Em7 to the Em13 chord in as many ways as you can. Think about it like you're adding a melody at the top of the chord voicing.

Here's just one simple example. Watch out for the 1/16th note rest on beat one. The strum is played with an up strum on the "e" of the "one e and a" count.

Example 7j:

One other common technique to use with this Em7 voicing is the hammer-on movement from an E11 chord to the Em7. This common decoration to the m7 sound is used all the time in funk, soul, disco and pop music.

The E11 chord is played like this (the hollow circle is optional):

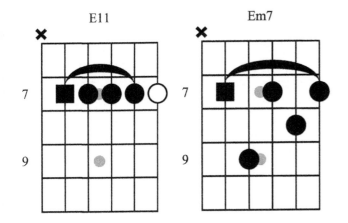

It is common to hammer on to an Em7 from this shape and you'll see this movement in the following example. Play the chord, then hammer your third and second fingers together to form the Em7 chord above.

Notice that the first strum is on the lower strings and the second strum (after the hammer on) is on the higher strings. Splitting up your chords in this way adds dynamics and depth to your guitar part.

Example 7k:

Here are a couple of musical examples that use this movement.

Example 7l:

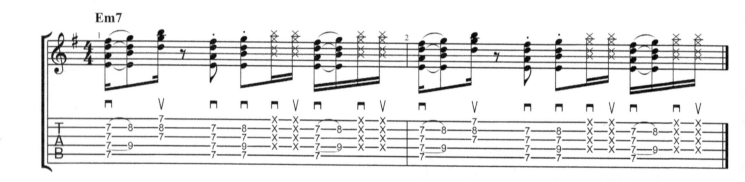

Note the movable Bm7 barre chord that slides down to Am7 in bar two:

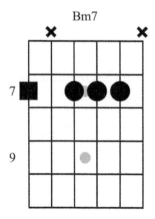

Example 7m:

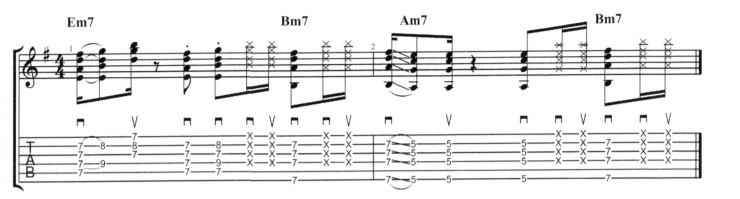

To round off this quick introduction to funk, here are five more important rhythm parts to give you a start for your own musical exploration. For more incredible funk ideas, check out our book **100 Essential Funk Grooves for Guitar** by Steve Allsworth.

Example 7n:

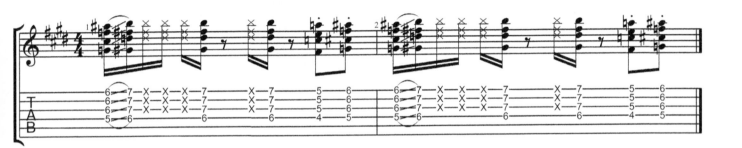

Example 7o:

Example 7p:

Example 7q:

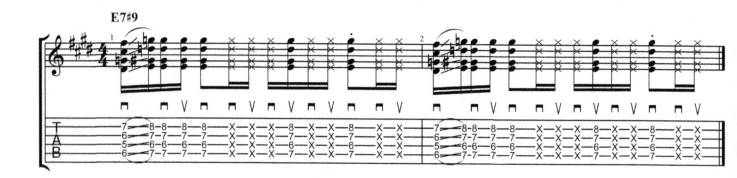

Example 7r:

Chapter Eight: Blues Triplets

All the rhythmic subdivisions we've studied so far split each beat into even numbers. However, it's common in many types of music to divide each beat into *three*. This type of music is said to have a *triplet* feel.

It might sound a little bit strange at first, but even though we split each of the four beats into three and create twelve subdivisions in a bar, these subdivisions are still called 1/8th notes. In fact, we write the *time signature* 12/8 at the beginning of the music to let performers know that there will be twelve 1/8th notes in each bar. These notes are phrased as four groups of three.

There are still four strong beats in each bar, they're just split into three instead of four.

On paper, it looks like this:

One of the most important types of music that frequently uses a triplet feel is the blues.

One simple way to play a blues rhythm guitar part is to strum only on each beat of the bar. Listen to this example and count "one two three, one two three, one two three, one two three" in each bar.

Example 8a:

We can add more interest by playing on each of the triplet subdivisions. Use down-strokes to strum the following pattern. When you're comfortable with playing this rhythm using all down strokes, try playing it with a **Down** Up Down, **Up** Down Up rhythm.

This will feel strange at first because every second beat will be played with an up stroke. It's one of the few times that your foot will be tapping down while your strum is moving up. It feels weird but stick with it as it's an important pattern to master.

Example 8b:

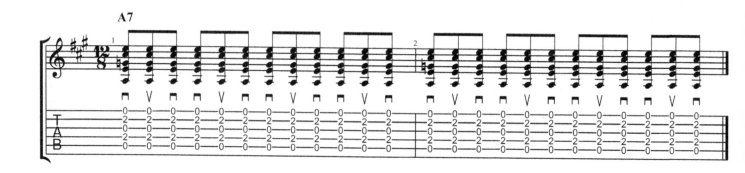

The previous example adds movement but it's very busy. Try playing only on the first and third triplet in each beat. Listen to the audio example if you're not sure how to play this idea. This rhythm is the basis of a "shuffle". Play this example as written at first, then repeat it allowing the first strum of each beat to ring out.

Example 8c:

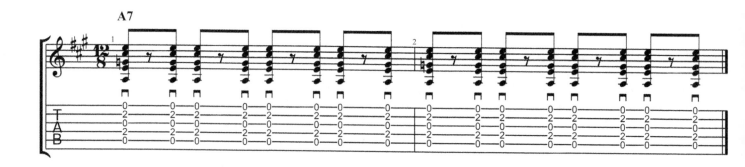

In most blues band situations, it's best to leave a lot of space in the rhythm guitar part. By playing sparsely, especially at the beginning of a tune, it gives the song room to grow. Here are some patterns that use the triplet rhythms but also leave large gaps that can be filled by other instruments.

Example 8d:

The next example is similar but misses out the first down strum in beat 4.

Example 8e:

Example 8f misses out the down strokes on beats 1, 3 and 4.

Example 8f:

The next idea is a little more challenging – you're only going to play the final triplet on each beat.

Example 8g:

Now we've looked at some of the most common blues triplet rhythms we can use them to play through a simple 12-bar blues sequence. If you've not come across a 12-bar blues before, one of the most common sequences is the one below. Begin by playing through with a 1/4 note strum on each beat.

Example 8h:

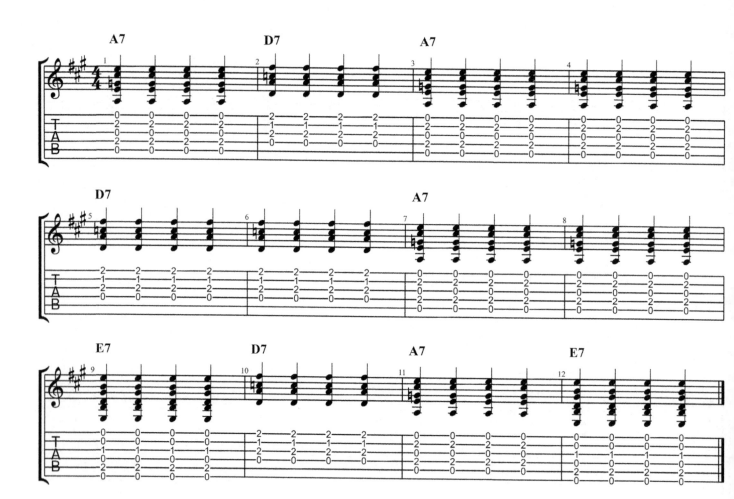

Now play it again using the strumming pattern from Example 8c. I've written out the first four bars for you here.

Example 8i:

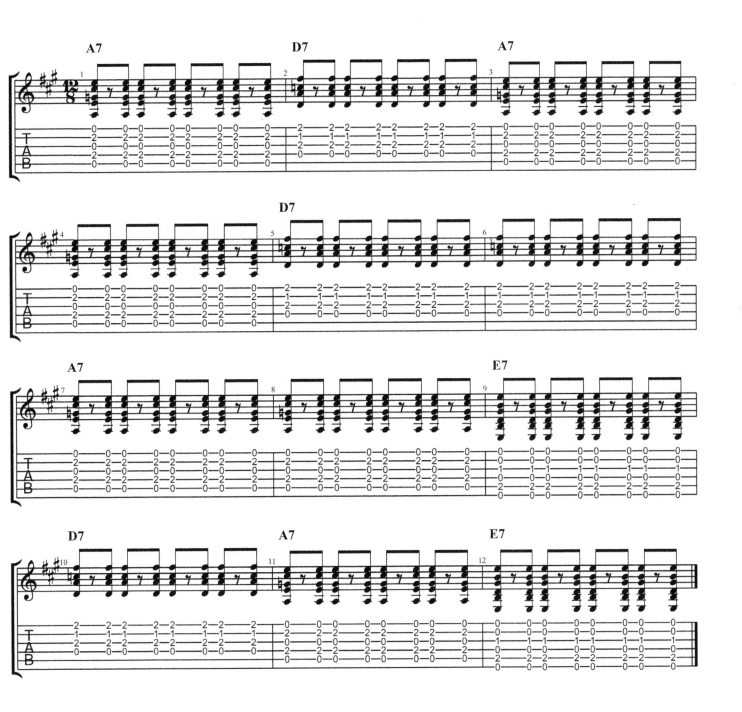

Now try it with the rhythm from Example 8e.

Example 8j:

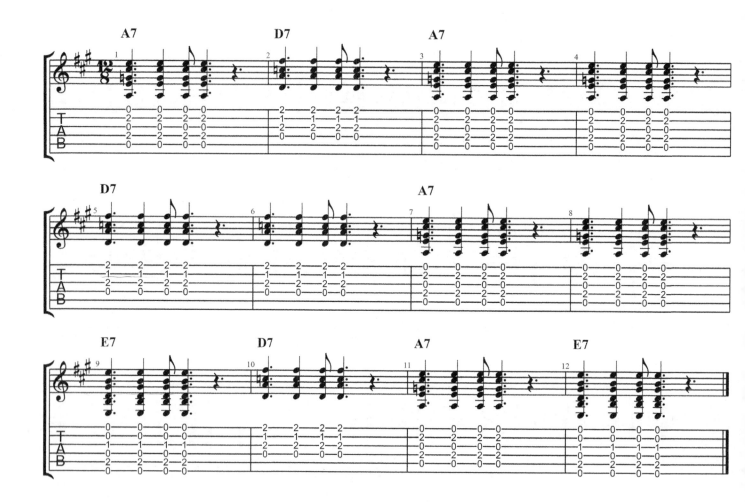

Now play through the 12-bar sequence using every rhythm you've covered in this chapter.

The Blues Boogie

Another important blues strumming pattern you should know is the blues boogie. It's created by holding down a chord then using another finger to add some movement. We'll learn it in the key of A.

Begin by holding down the 2nd fret of the fourth string with your first finger and strumming the fifth and fourth strings twice to play a mini A chord. Next, without removing your first finger, place your third finger on the fourth fret and play the two strings again twice. Repeat the whole figure to fill out a bar.

Example 8k shows the basic blues boogie feel played on an A chord for two bars. Pay attention to the timing. The first strum of each pair lasts for the first two 1/8th notes in the beat, the second strum is played on the final 1/18th note. This creates an almost swung shuffle feel.

Example 8k:

Here's the same pattern on a D chord.

Example 8l:

And here's the same pattern on an E chord. We now have the three chords we need to play a full 12-bar blues.

Example 8m:

Use these three chords to play through the whole blues progression.

Example 8n:

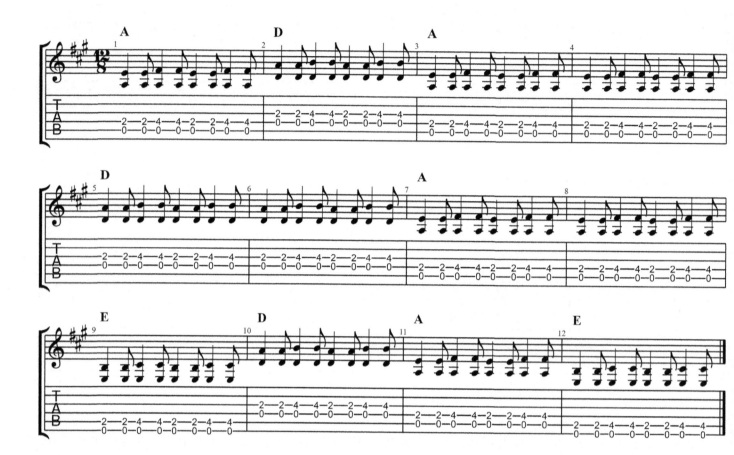

This simple pattern adds great depth to the guitar part when we play blues rhythm and is much more interesting than simply playing chords.

There are variations to the basic pattern that can be inserted anywhere to add even more interest and variation. Subtle variations in the rhythm guitar part can help give the soloist creative ideas and build the groove of the music for both the band and the audience.

In this example use your *little finger* to stretch out and play the 5th fret of the fourth string on beat 3. Move this idea through the chord changes as we did in Example 8n.

Example 8o:

The next variation adds a hammer-on idea on the fifth string

Example 8p:

Another classic riff in the style of John Lee Hooker uses "pull-offs" to create a descending bassline at the end of each bar.

Example 8q:

Until now, the bass fills have taken place on the final few beats of each bar. We can easily shake things up a bit by adding a fill on beat 2.

Example 8r:

A great approach is to split each chord into two parts to *displace* the bassline.

Example 8s:

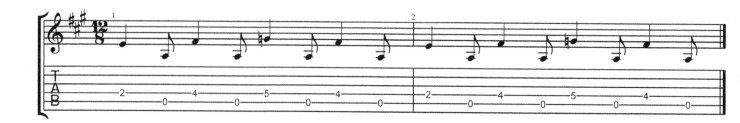

Once you have a few of these riffs under your fingers, mix and match them in a 12-bar blues progression. All the ideas are freely interchangeable so slot them in wherever you feel they work.

One possible example out of the thousands of permutations is shown below. I've added a couple of new fills to keep you on your toes!

Example 8t:

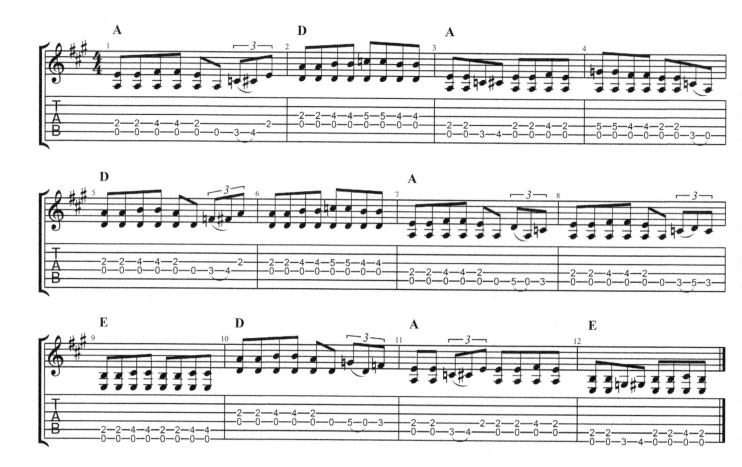

For hundreds more blues guitar rhythm patterns, check out my book **The Complete Guide to Blues Guitar: Rhythm**.

Conclusion

So, there we have it – a detailed introduction to rhythm and strumming – one of the most important skills in guitar. We've covered the nuts and bolts of how rhythms are created, played, embellished and, most importantly, made to groove with pushed and pulled accents.

The material we've covered will form the core of your strumming arsenal in any style of music and enable you to play pretty much any rhythm you come across in your musical journey.

From here, your job is to go and listen to as much music in your favourite genre as possible, to hear the kinds of strumming patterns that are used to create the right vibe. As you listen, mute the strings of your guitar and try to recreate the strumming patterns you hear. This will help to internalise the rhythms and they will become part of your own natural vocabulary, just like learning a new word from a book.

Try using these patterns with different chord sequences and quickly you'll be writing your own unique songs. The sky is the limit, so don't be afraid to borrow ideas from different musicians and combine them to create your own unique voice.

The most important thing is to have fun while you experiment and develop your musical ears.

Good luck on your journey!

Joseph

How To Play Guitar – 3 in 1 Beginner Series

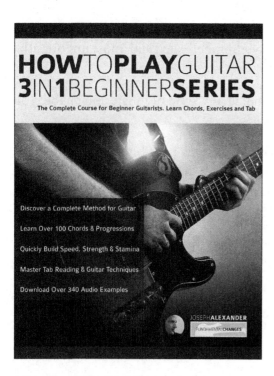

This How to Play Guitar box set contains three best-selling titles that have helped over 100,000 students learn to play guitar. It contains the three beginner guitar methods:

- *How to Read Guitar Tablature*

- *The First 100 Chords for Guitar*

- *The First 100 Guitar Exercises for Beginners*

Together, they form a complete course that will take you from zero to hero as you learn to play the guitar. Discover how to read guitar tab, play essential chords, write chord progressions, and build your fluency and speed on the guitar.

How to Read Guitar Tablature is the ideal music stand companion and gig bag essential. Never be confused again by the odd signs and abbreviations that appear in tab, and expand your technique repertoire as you learn!

The First 100 Chords for Guitar is not simply a cold list of chords, it's a complete guitar method for beginners that teaches you how to practice for a lifetime of good guitar habits.

From the most basic chords, right through to some rich and exciting advanced voicings, you will learn to play guitar in small friendly steps. Throughout, there is an emphasis on using the correct fingers, changing chords smoothly, building great technique, and developing your own creativity.

The First 100 Guitar Exercises for Beginners is the quickest way to build technique, control, strength, stamina and speed on the guitar.

Unlike some books that take a "technical drill" approach, this book gets you playing real music right away. Why practice boring exercise you'll never want to play again? This is a method that combines learning the technique of the guitar with the fun of playing music.

Discover a proven system that teaches you rapid, musical progress on guitar, and how play songs in no time. It's the first step on your path to total beginner guitar mastery.

Buy it now to get access to some of the best teachers, lessons and exercises in the world… and save money while you're at it!

Printed in Great Britain
by Amazon

42615908R00046